Text, illustrations, and typeface ©1995 by Lizi Boyd.

All rights reserved.

Typeset in Boydfont.

Book design by Laura Lovett.

Printed in Hong Kong.

ISBN 0-8118-0780-0

Distributed in Canada by Raincoast Books

8680 Cambie Street, Vancouver, B.C. V6P 6M9

10 9 8 7 6 5 4 3

Chronicle Books

85 Second Street, San Francisco, California 94105

BABY'S JOURNAL
A Book of Firsts

Lizi Boyd

Chronicle Books San Francisco

Dreaming of Baby

What we thought you'd be like

Baby-Belly Photo

or Mama & Papa before
Baby was born

Baby Shower

Who threw it:

Guests:

Gifts:

The Nursery

Getting ready for Baby

Baby Joins Our World

Time:

Date:

Weight:

Height:

Doctor/Midwife:

Baby looks like:

Baby Announcement

paste here

Naming You

Baby's First Photo

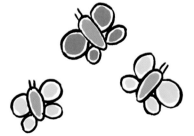

The Tree Grows

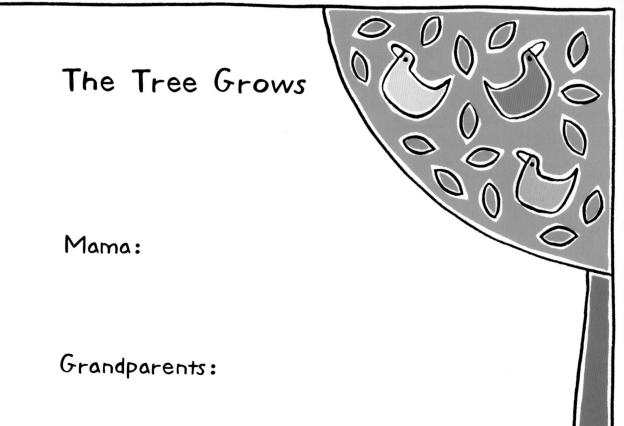

Mama:

Grandparents:

Great-grandparents:

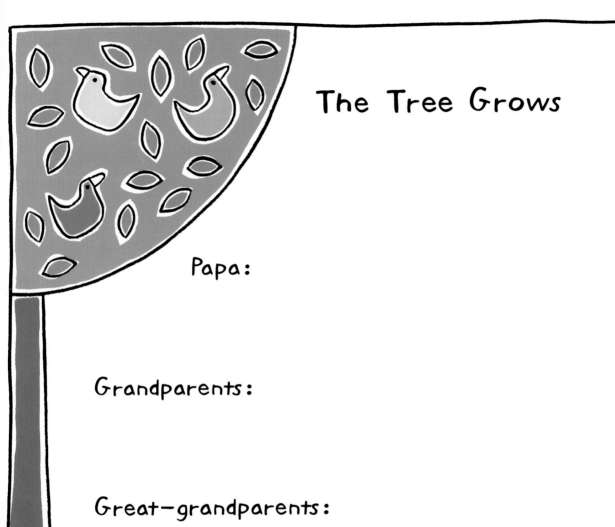

The Tree Grows

Papa:

Grandparents:

Great-grandparents:

Family Photo

First Cozy
Moments

Going Home

Date:

Address:

Baby meets:

Flowers & surprises:

Celebrations

Baby Sees, Hears, Discovers

Lullabies, Naps, and Nights

Baby's First Smile

Baby's Smiley Photo

Baby's Sounds
Cooing, giggling, babbling

Baby's Baths

Baby's
First Outings

Adventures
& Travel

Baby Rolls Over!

Baby Sits Up

Favorite Baby Faces

Baby Face Photo

Baby Play

Baby Giggles

What makes Baby laugh

Favorite
Books & Toys

Special Hats & Clothes

Oh! Crawling Baby

Baby's Comforts

Favorite blanket, animal, object:

Then There Came Teeth

Baby's first tooth:

Baby's second tooth:

Baby Joins Us at the Table

Favorite foods:

Dislikes:

Baby's Friends

Baby and Friend Photo

One Step, Two Steps, Walking!

Go-Baby-Go Photo

Waving Baby

First real wave:

First real kisses:

Favorite Walks

Baby's First Phone Call

Dancing Baby

Favorite music & songs:

Baby's First Birthday

Birthday Photo

Baby's First Haircut

Lock of Baby's hair

Days & Ways with Papa

Papa & Baby Photo

Days & Ways with Mama

Mama & Baby Photo

Oh Holidays!

Oh Holidays!

I Remember When Baby . . .

Baby's First Words

Stellar Moments

Our Wishes for Baby

Now that we know you, our wishes are: